UNPLUG

BREATHE

CREATE

A MONTH OF HONING
YOUR ZONE OF GENIUS
THROUGH MEDITATION

Unplug Breathe Create: A Month of Honing Your Zone of Genius Through Meditation is a work of my own creation.

The information in this book was correct at the time of publication, and the Author does not assume any liability for loss or damage caused by errors or omissions, again, this is my perspective, opinion, and experience, so it has been written as such.

ISBN - 979-8-9875738-9-1

Cover, Book Design, and Layout by megs thompson, megswrites llc
www.megswrites.com

www.inomniaparatuspublishing.com

"THE GOAL IN LIFE IS NOT TO ATTAIN SOME IMAGINARY IDEAL; IT IS TO FIND AND FULLY USE OUR OWN GIFTS."

—GAY HENDRICKS

This journal is part of the
UNPLUG BREATHE CREATE
series & designed to be used
alongside a bespoke guided
meditation.

Download this month's meditation
using the QR code below:

HOW TO BEST USE THIS JOURNAL & MEDITATION

UNPLUG

The first step to reconnecting with ourselves as creative beings is to unplug & disconnect even temporarily from the countless electronic tethers that keep us firmly held in the world of shoulds & must's.

BREATHE

Take a few deep breaths, paying close attention to the way oxygen moves through your mouth & nose, filling your lungs & reawakening the creative genius locked safely within you, exhaling any fears, hesitations, or doubts that may filter your magic.

CREATE

Release your desire to control, plan & perfect every step & movement you make. Embrace the often wild, messy & chaotic magic that comes with allowing your inner creative to explore & play. Prepare yourself to experience fulfillment & satisfaction in new & creative ways.

DAILY ROUTINE

    While moving through your day, begin implementing the use of affirmations. Both habits & beliefs are formed & strengthened through consistent repetition & before you know it your thoughts will become truths.

    Included below are powerful affirmations that when paired with your daily tasks & activities, will empower you through this month of finding & claiming your own creative space.

    I recommend repeating one or more of these affirmations aloud anytime you find yourself in front of a mirror, washing your hands, or refilling your beverage of choice.

I AM MAKING A POWERFUL IMPACT EVERY SINGLE DAY.

I TAP INTO MY UNIQUE ZONE OF GENIUS WITH CONFIDENCE & EASE.

I APPROACH LIFE WITHOUT HESITATION OR APOLOGY.

30-DAY ENERGY TRACKER

When you've completed your daily meditation, make note of a single word or phrase that best describes your energy level in that moment.

Day 1	Day 2	Day 3	Day 4	Day 5
Day 6	Day 7	Day 8	Day 9	Day 10
Day 11	Day 12	Day 13	Day 14	Day 15
Day 16	Day 17	Day 18	Day 19	Day 20
Day 21	Day 22	Day 23	Day 24	Day 25
Day 26	Day 27	Day 28	Day 29	Day 30

DAY 1

During the meditation you visualized a hallway with framed documents, accolades & notes of recognition. What did some of them say? Who were they from? What are some of the most recent pieces of feedback & praise you've received from your clients, colleagues & friends?

_____

_____

_____

_____

_____

_____

_____

_____

_____

_____

_____

_____

_____

_____

_____

_____

_____

ON A SCALE OF 1-5 WHAT'S YOUR
CURRENT CREATIVITY LEVEL?

DAY 2

Looking back at your journaling from yesterday, how do you feel when you receive these expressions of gratitude, appreciation & recognition for your expertise?

ON A SCALE OF 1-5 WHAT'S YOUR
CURRENT CREATIVITY LEVEL?

DAY 3

When you viewed your reflection in the mirror, what colors did you see glowing from your heart, soul & spirit? What do you associate those colors with? How do they make you feel?

_____

_____

_____

_____

_____

_____

_____

_____

_____

_____

_____

_____

_____

_____

_____

ON A SCALE OF 1-5 WHAT'S YOUR
CURRENT CREATIVITY LEVEL?

DAY 4

What skills, hobbies, projects & accomplishments
seem to break the rules of time & space for you?
These are the tasks or practices you can spend hours
focused on, without feeling like any time has passed.

_____

_____

_____

_____

_____

_____

_____

_____

_____

_____

_____

_____

_____

_____

_____

_____

_____

_____

ON A SCALE OF 1-5 WHAT'S YOUR
CURRENT CREATIVITY LEVEL?

DAY 5

Revisiting your journaling from yesterday, how often are you finding time to spend on the tasks, projects & practices that you wrote about? The ones where you can lose yourself for hours without feeling like any time has passed.

ON A SCALE OF 1-5 WHAT'S YOUR
CURRENT CREATIVITY LEVEL?

DAY 6

Where in your life do you feel most aligned, fulfilled, complete & powerful? What situations, experiences, people, projects help promote this feeling?

_____

_____

_____

_____

_____

_____

_____

_____

_____

_____

_____

_____

_____

_____

_____

_____

_____

ON A SCALE OF 1-5 WHAT'S YOUR
CURRENT CREATIVITY LEVEL?

DAY 7

Often we confuse our zone of excellence with our zone of genius. Our zone of excellence is comprised of the activities that we're skilled at, but don't necessarily love doing. What do you see as being your zone or zones of excellence?

_____

_____

_____

_____

_____

_____

_____

_____

_____

_____

_____

_____

_____

_____

_____

ON A SCALE OF 1-5 WHAT'S YOUR
CURRENT CREATIVITY LEVEL?

DAY 8

Our zone of genius is comprised of the activities that we're uniquely skilled at & that we love to do, so much so, that time and space disappear when we're doing them. What do you see as being your zone or zones of genius?

ON A SCALE OF 1-5 WHAT'S YOUR
CURRENT CREATIVITY LEVEL?

DAY 9

How are you currently leaning into you zone(s) of genius in your daily life, both personal & professional? How might you be able to increase this?

ON A SCALE OF 1-5 WHAT'S YOUR
CURRENT CREATIVITY LEVEL?

DAY 10

Many times we don't recognize that our zone of genius is an extension of our zone of creativity. For example: if your zone of genius is writing powerful content with ease, your zone of creativity may be writing & sharing stories for children & adults. How might your zone of genius translate into your zone of creativity?

ON A SCALE OF 1-5 WHAT'S YOUR
CURRENT CREATIVITY LEVEL?

DAY 11

Our zone of genius is where we're able to enter a flow of infinite creativity & transcend time. What areas of your current life feel like work & seem to drag on? These tasks are likely not fulfilling your soul's purpose, but may be a step on your journey to something better.

_____

_____

_____

_____

_____

_____

_____

_____

_____

_____

_____

_____

_____

_____

ON A SCALE OF 1-5 WHAT'S YOUR
CURRENT CREATIVITY LEVEL?

DAY 12

In what ways might you be able to shift the areas & tasks of your daily life that feel like work, to better align with your unique zone of genius?

_____

_____

_____

_____

_____

_____

_____

_____

_____

_____

_____

_____

_____

_____

_____

_____

_____

ON A SCALE OF 1-5 WHAT'S YOUR
CURRENT CREATIVITY LEVEL?

DAY 13

Do you have colleagues or teammates that have a complimentary zone of genius to yours? Are there areas of your daily life that can be delegated to them, and vice versa, so that you can both work within your zones of genius?

_____

_____

_____

_____

_____

_____

_____

_____

_____

_____

_____

_____

_____

_____

ON A SCALE OF 1-5 WHAT'S YOUR
CURRENT CREATIVITY LEVEL?

DAY 14

Reflecting back on your musings from yesterday.
What hesitations do you feel around asking for
support? When you do delegate tasks to others, are
you able to let go of your attachment to the task, or
do you continue to find it taking up space in your
mind?

ON A SCALE OF 1-5 WHAT'S YOUR
CURRENT CREATIVITY LEVEL?

DAY 15

How did you most enjoy expressing yourself
creatively as a child, before you began experiencing
the expectations & shoulds that come with being an
adult? Is there a way for you to bring this into your
life & responsibilities now?

ON A SCALE OF 1-5 WHAT'S YOUR
CURRENT CREATIVITY LEVEL?

DAY 16

What resistance or fears do you feel around the idea of sharing your zone of genius with others? Are these feelings based in past experiences or assumptions?

ON A SCALE OF 1-5 WHAT'S YOUR
CURRENT CREATIVITY LEVEL?

DAY 17

What do you consider to be your unique creative strengths? How would you describe these strengths to others? Are these skills you were taught by someone else or learned through self-discovery?

_____

_____

_____

_____

_____

_____

_____

_____

_____

_____

_____

_____

_____

_____

_____

_____

_____

ON A SCALE OF 1-5 WHAT'S YOUR
CURRENT CREATIVITY LEVEL?

DAY 18

What is one task that you complete every day. This may be something mundane, administrative & without much sparkle. How can you approach this task from a more creative standpoint, leaning into your zone of genius?

ON A SCALE OF 1-5 WHAT'S YOUR
CURRENT CREATIVITY LEVEL?

DAY 19

What limiting beliefs do you hold when it comes to
exploring your own creativity & zone of genius?
Where did these beliefs originate?

ON A SCALE OF 1-5 WHAT'S YOUR
CURRENT CREATIVITY LEVEL?

DAY 20

How often do you allow yourself to embrace your own
creativity & zone of genius? What's holding you back
from prioritizing this time? As with any habit or skill,
consistent repetition strengthens & solidifies your
confidence as a creative being. Are you able to set
aside 10, 20, or even 30 minutes each day to explore
approaching daily tasks from you zone of genius?

ON A SCALE OF 1-5 WHAT'S YOUR
CURRENT CREATIVITY LEVEL?

DAY 21

What is one problem or roadblock that you're experiencing? This may be something small or large. How can you approach this issue by tapping into your unique zone of genius?

_____

_____

_____

_____

_____

_____

_____

_____

_____

_____

_____

_____

_____

_____

_____

_____

_____

ON A SCALE OF 1-5 WHAT'S YOUR
CURRENT CREATIVITY LEVEL?

DAY 22

What lights you up? What topics or areas in life are you most passionate about? How do you currently use your creativity in these areas? How might you be able to better tap into your creativity & zone of genius?

ON A SCALE OF 1-5 WHAT'S YOUR
CURRENT CREATIVITY LEVEL?

DAY 23

Reflect on a recently completed project. Something you accomplished successfully & are proud of. How might that project have been even stronger, better, more impactful by utilizing your creativity & zone of genius?

ON A SCALE OF 1-5 WHAT'S YOUR
CURRENT CREATIVITY LEVEL?

DAY 24

When do you feel most empowered & confident? In what situations? With what people? In what tasks or environments? Many of the answers you find here will help in honing your unique zone of genius, as well as how you might better lean into your authentic purpose.

ON A SCALE OF 1-5 WHAT'S YOUR
CURRENT CREATIVITY LEVEL?

DAY 25

What does satisfaction look like to you? How does it feel? Where in your body do you feel satisfaction?

ON A SCALE OF 1-5 WHAT'S YOUR
CURRENT CREATIVITY LEVEL?

DAY 26

How would you choose to creatively express yourself today, if time & money weren't factors? What's holding you back from doing so? Is it truly time, money, a fear of failure, or something else?

_____

_____

_____

_____

_____

_____

_____

_____

_____

_____

_____

_____

_____

_____

_____

_____

ON A SCALE OF 1-5 WHAT'S YOUR
CURRENT CREATIVITY LEVEL?

DAY 27

How might you introduce yourself & your unique zone of genius to a new acquaintance in a more creative way? Perhaps through a short story, a poem, a picture, a graphic, a song, or something else?

_____

_____

_____

_____

_____

_____

_____

_____

_____

_____

_____

_____

_____

_____

_____

_____

_____

ON A SCALE OF 1-5 WHAT'S YOUR
CURRENT CREATIVITY LEVEL?

DAY 28

When do you feel most like a genius? Where in your body do you feel this? How would you describe this feeling or sensation? How might you be able to creatively amplify this feeling?

ON A SCALE OF 1-5 WHAT'S YOUR
CURRENT CREATIVITY LEVEL?

DAY 29

What are 3 aspects of your daily life that feel most aligned & bring you the most joy? How might you amplify these areas to better share your unique zone of genius with others?

_____

_____

_____

_____

_____

_____

_____

_____

_____

_____

_____

_____

_____

_____

_____

_____

ON A SCALE OF 1-5 WHAT'S YOUR
CURRENT CREATIVITY LEVEL?

DAY 30

Describe your unique zone of genius as a superpower. Write a brief story that showcases who you are, how your superpower helps you to thwart the opposition & the good you're able to spread to the world by leaning into your natural abilities.

ON A SCALE OF 1-5 WHAT'S YOUR
CURRENT CREATIVITY LEVEL?

If you already have an UNPLUG BREATHE CREATE subscription, keep an eye on your mailbox for your next delivery.

If you aren't yet a member but would like to be, or are interested in gifting a membership to someone else, scan the QR code below.